POL

Margaret Mead

by Michael Pollard

Picture Credits:
Courtesy Department Library Services American Museum of Natural History: 40 (Photo P.E. Logan), 50; The Bettmann Archive: 47; Black Star/Colorific!: 60; Compix: 11; Sally and Richard Greenhill: 28; Robert Harding Picture Library: 6, 7 (top), 42, 43 (top), 52; Ken Heyman: cover; Hulton Picture Company/The Bettmann Archive: 23 (both); The Hutchison Library: 7 (below left and right), 14, 20 (both), 29 (below), 32 (both), 34, 35, 43 (below), 49; Courtesy of the Institute for Intercultural Studies, Inc., New York: 4, 9, 10, 17 (below), 19, 26, 31, 36-7, 39, 45 (both), 59; Royal Geographical Society Picture Library: 13; ZEFA: 17 (top), 24, 25, 29 (top), 56 (both), 57.

Published in Great Britain in 1992
by Exley Publications Ltd,
16 Chalk Hill, Watford,
Herts WD1 4BN, United Kingdom.

A copy of the CIP data is available from
the British Library on request.

ISBN 1-85015-258-6

Series editor: Helen Exley.
Picture research: Caroline Mitchell.
Editorial: Margaret Montgomery.
Typeset by Brush Off Studios,
St Albans.
Printed and bound in Hungary.

Margaret Mead

*The famous anthropologist who
helped people all over the world
to understand each other's cultures*

Michael Pollard

The way we are

Why do we behave in the way we do? What makes some of us cheerful and others miserable, some quarrelsome and others friendly, some helpful and others hard to please? Are we born like that, or do we become like it as we grow up?

Where do we get our ideas of what's right or wrong, fair or unfair, beautiful or ugly? Are we born with them, or do we get them from our parents and other people around us?

These are questions that scientists who study the way people behave have been asking for nearly 150 years. In 1859, the British scientist Charles Darwin published his famous book, *The Origin of Species*. This put forward the idea of "natural selection". In man and in all other living things, Darwin wrote, the healthier and more successful specimens survived and bred while the weaker ones died out. If there were more strong specimens than weak ones, the species grew in numbers. If not, it began to disappear. In other words, the ability to survive was passed on from one generation to the next – from parents to their children.

It was not long before scientists were wondering whether other things could be passed on in this way. Could it be that there were families in which crime was passed from parents to children in the same way as the ability to survive? Some people went further. What about kindness, or good manners or bad temper?

There is no easy answer. It very often seems that children have the good or bad habits of their parents. But were they born with those habits, or did they pick them up by imitation? How much do we copy the way other people around us behave,

Opposite: Margaret Mead (on the left) photographed on her first field trip in Samoa in 1925. She is with Fa'amotu, a Samoan chief's daughter who introduced her to local food and customs. Margaret is wearing what she described as "a sarong-like garment which I could slip off under the village shower as I slipped a dry one on."

5

or people we see in films or on television? People still argue about these questions today.

In the 1920s the arguments were even louder. There were a number of reasons for this. In North America and Europe, free education for all had been introduced fifty or more years before. It was expected to lead to a better, less violent society. This hadn't happened. Was there, some people asked, something wrong with the way children were educated – and if so, was this because no one understood how children learn?

Nature or nurture?

At the same time, there was an outbreak of concern about "reckless and rebellious youth". Public worries on this topic were not new, but they had increased because of the possible influence of the cinema and radio on young people. One question that was being asked was whether American parents

Above, left and opposite: "This is who I am." Decorating their bodies is one way in which people of many cultures express their identity and sometimes their status. Anthropologists are interested in how important the way people behave is and what it means.

were raising their children in a way (including letting them go to the cinema) that made them "reckless and rebellious" as teenagers, or whether the children were born rebels. Today, worries about the influence of television have replaced those about the cinema, but no one has been able to prove that films or television affect the way people behave.

"Nature or nurture" is a shorthand way of describing the argument. Some people say that "nature" is the most important guide to someone's character and the way he or she behaves. They believe that children receive their characters from their parents and their grandparents in the same way as they receive their physical characteristics. Those who believe in "nurture" think that the influence of the family and the outside world is more important.

Anthropology

The "nature or nurture" question is of great interest to anthropologists. Anthropology is the study of humans as a species and anthropologists are concerned with how different physical types of people have evolved. For example, why are the pygmies of Central Africa so small and the aborigines of Australia so tall? Anthropologists are interested in how groups of people – societies – relate to their surroundings. They study how societies make sense of the world through family relationships, religion, language and the arts. And they try to understand the ways in which families and communities work.

Among the scientists interested in "nature or nurture" was Professor Franz Boas, head of the Department of Anthropology of Columbia University in New York. One of his students in the early 1920s was a lively, but serious minded, young woman, Margaret Mead.

By 1925, Margaret, aged twenty-three, had a master's degree in psychology, the study of the mind. She was about to receive her doctorate in anthropology. Having spent five years studying, she wanted to get out of the lecture hall and do some research. Anthropology is a science where books and lectures can take the student only so far. The real work must be done "in the field" – that is, living closely with the people being studied. This presented Franz Boas with a problem.

A test of strength

Born on December 16, 1901, Margaret Mead had lived a sheltered, middle-class life. Her father was a university professor. Her mother was a campaigner for good causes such as civil rights for black people and women, and the plight of immigrants to the United States. Margaret had never been to a foreign country and spoke no foreign languages. She had never taken a sea voyage or even stayed in an hotel. In all her life, she had never spent a whole day on her own. What was more, she had married as a student. Her husband, Luther Cressman, intended at that time to make his career in the Church.

Despite all this, Margaret was determined to carry on in the field with the study she had already started at university. This was of the culture of Polynesia, the islands of the South Pacific. Civilization was reaching out to the islands. Soon, their old customs and way of life would have vanished for ever. Margaret wanted to observe and record them before they disappeared.

Boas was horrified. Could he take the responsibility of giving this young woman permission to travel half-way across the world, to islands where she might meet fearful danger or deadly disease, where there were said to be cannibals and headhunters? What would he say to her husband and her parents if anything happened to her? And the islands on which she had set her heart on going to, the Tuamotu Islands in French Polynesia, were among the most remote, with only rare and chancy contacts with the outside world.

Today, it's not unusual for a young woman to travel the world after leaving university and before starting on a career. In the 1920s, it was almost unheard-of for a woman of any age to travel alone,

"I was always glad that I was a girl. I cannot remember ever wanting to be a boy. It seems to me this was because of the way I was treated by my parents. I was a wanted child, and when I was born I was the kind of child my parents wanted."

Margaret Mead,
from her autobiography,
"Blackberry Winter".

Margaret with her brother Richard, who was born when she was two. Margaret was the eldest of five children.

except on luxury liners along well-known routes. It was almost as unusual for a woman – especially a married woman – to be planning a career. In those days, married women were expected to settle down, make a home and have children. Margaret seemed determined to break all the rules.

Why not, Boas suggested to her, make a study of native American Indian culture instead? This would be just as interesting. It could be done in surroundings which were less dangerous and closer to home. The Indian reservations had good communications if anything were to go wrong.

Wanderlust

It may also have been in Franz Boas's mind that a spell of field work among the Indian people would cure Margaret of her wanderlust and she would choose a university-based career instead. No, Margaret insisted. American Indian culture had already been spoilt by contact with white Americans. The changes she wanted to study were already over for the native American Indians. In the South Pacific, change had not arrived or had only just begun. She wanted to go where an old culture still lived on, to a place that had not been invaded by modern ideas. To the Tuamotu Islands in the Pacific Ocean, for example.

Franz Boas knew that Margaret was a brilliant student who deserved to be given a chance to make a name for herself. He wanted her to research the subject that was very much in the news – the way teenagers behave. She wanted to make a wider study. She wanted to know what happened in a culture when civilization brought change. This was to be her lifelong interest.

Boas and his prize student accepted a compromise. She was not interested in studying the American Indians. But she would not insist on Tuamotu, if Boas would let her go somewhere else in the South Pacific. And she would accept his idea of studying the way adolescents behave – particularly girls – instead of her own proposal.

Margaret, aged twenty-four, just before her departure to Samoa. At a conference of anthropologists in Toronto, Canada a year before, she had made her decision to start field work as soon as she could. What she had heard at the conference convinced her that there was no time to be lost if vanishing cultures were to be studied and recorded.

Off to Samoa

After some searching, a suitable place was found – Samoa, a group of South Pacific islands about one thousand miles south of the equator. Discovered in the eighteenth century, the islands had become important trading posts. Later, they became ports of call for steamships to take on fuel and other supplies.

By 1925, the group of islands had been divided in two. Western Samoa, today an independent state, was administered by New Zealand. The eastern half, American Samoa, was and still is United States territory. The United States Navy had a large base, with a hospital and a radio station, at Pago Pago on the island of Tutuila.

The American base was the reason for Boas's agreement that Margaret Mead could work there. If she found herself in any trouble, he reasoned, she would be able to turn to the United States Navy for help. Also, there was a regular passenger service to Pago Pago every three weeks, and civilians could

Fishing was – and still is – a vital industry in Samoa. In this fishing village, the nets are hung out to dry. A few weeks after Margaret's arrival in the islands, a hurricane destroyed many of the villagers' homes and boats. Margaret's field work was held up because everyone was too busy rebuilding their houses, repairing their boats and making new nets.

send or receive cable messages through the radio station. So on August 31, 1925, Margaret Mead arrived in Samoa aboard the *SS Sonoma* after a three-thousand mile voyage from Hawaii.

In at the deep end

A scientist going on such an expedition today would travel in a group which would include specialists in different, appropriate subjects. They would take vast quantities of equipment, including emergency medical supplies, measuring instruments, storage for samples, typewriters, tape-recorders, film, video and still cameras, film lighting, electric generators and their own transport.

Margaret's equipment was far more basic: apart from personal luggage, it consisted of pencils, notebooks, a camera and a spare pair of glasses. And she was alone. There would be no chance of discussing her research except through letters to Franz Boas and colleagues such as Ruth Benedict, Boas's assistant and Margaret's lifelong friend.

In those days, scientists going to work in the field received no training in methods of observing and recording their findings. No one asked whether they could stand the loneliness of field work or how they would cope with possible danger. It was a case of throwing field workers in at the deep end and finding out whether they could swim. "Many who are now professors teach their students as their professors taught them," Margaret Mead wrote later, "and if young fieldworkers do not give up in despair, go mad, ruin their health or die, they do, after a fashion, become anthropologists. But it is a wasteful system, a system I have no time for."

Later in her life, she gave a great deal of her time to training field workers and helping them to live with the problems they might meet.

Remote though the Pacific islands were in the days before scheduled air services, a good deal was known about them in North America and Europe. Sailors, missionaries and explorers had brought back reports of life in the islands. More recently, the South Seas, as the southern Pacific was then

NATIVES SAVII

generally called, had become a place of romantic pilgrimage for many European writers and artists. The French impressionist painter, Gauguin, had spent the last twelve years of his life at Tahiti, one of the Windward Islands, and in the Marquesas. The Scottish novelist, Robert Louis Stevenson, lived for seven years – and died – in Samoa, and wrote three books about his experiences.

The popular picture of the Polynesian people that had emerged was of simple, friendly people with gracious movements and smiling faces. The English poet, Rupert Brooke, who had also lived in Samoa, had described the Samoans as "the loveliest people in the world, moving and running and dancing like gods and goddesses." No wonder that some of Margaret's envious colleagues told her that she was "setting off for heaven."

A Samoan family set out for a fishing expedition in their canoe. Margaret enjoyed many fishing trips in Samoa, and found that it was the boys who were the experts, although they were noisy. "When a fish is seen there is much hallooing," she wrote home. "The fishing is all very inefficient and festive."

13

First impressions

But Margaret's first impressions on her arrival at Pago Pago were disappointing. The port was noisy with naval aircraft and ships' bands playing ragtime. She was depressed to see how the United States Navy had introduced American culture and values to the Samoans. The women were dressed, not in the traditional costumes, but in "various hideous striped American stuffs." She felt ashamed of her own country's influence on the people.

Over the next few weeks, Margaret visited most of the villages on Tutuila. The villages on bus routes, she found, had been "very much influenced by American goods and American visitors and do not present a typical picture of the original culture." None of the villages had enough teenage girls to make a suitable group for research.

"Because of these disadvantages," she wrote to Boas, "I have decided to go to Ta'u, one of three small islands in the Manu'a group about one hundred miles from here." There, she explained, she would be able to live with the only white family on the island.

Edward Holt was a United States Navy man in charge of the dispensary, and lived in a European-style house with his wife Ruth and their children. There was a spare room for Margaret, and a small house nearby where she could' interview the Samoan girls from Ta'u's four villages. In November, having struggled to learn the Samoan language, she set out for Ta'u, where she was to spend the next six months.

Margaret immediately felt more cheerful once she was in Ta'u, though the climate was much hotter. The island was one hundred miles nearer the equator than Pago Pago, and no work was possible in the middle of the day. Ta'u proved, as she had been told, "much more primitive and unspoiled than any other part of Samoa", and she was soon observing and recording Polynesian dances and spending time with native families.

By January, she was able to report that "gradually I am becoming part of the community." She had learnt the trick of obtaining information from the

Opposite: Dancing was an important part of the evening routine that Margaret observed in Samoa. First, everyone bathed in the sea. Then, after evening prayers, the children began dancing. After supper, the dancing continued. Individuals and groups made up their own dances while the adults loudly praised or criticized their efforts.

"There is no way of knowing in advance what the people will be like or even what they will look like. There may be photographs of them, but by the time one arrives they may look different.... One doesn't know where one will live or what there will be to eat or whether it will turn out a good thing to have rubber boots, mosquito boots, sandals that keep one's feet cool, or woollen socks to absorb the sweat."

Margaret Mead on field work, from her autobiography, "Blackberry Winter".

villagers. Sitting down with them and asking questions involved a ritual of exchanging small gifts. The Samoans gave Margaret shells and flowers, and her gifts were writing-paper, envelopes, needles and thread. She also became a "fixer" for the village people, writing letters for them, obtaining things they wanted through the Navy store, and taking photographs for them.

It was an eventful six months. Soon after her arrival, a hurricane devastated the village where she was living. Visits to the other villages could involve wading for miles with mud up to her knees. There were mosquitoes everywhere. One morning she killed thirty-five inside her mosquito net. "All had dined liberally – a quaint way of dipping one's hands in one's own blood."

Margaret carried out her research in a spare house near the dispensary. She interviewed the girls of the village, tested their intelligence and recorded their experiences and family background.

Confusion and uncertainty

When she returned to Pago Pago on her way home in May 1926 she had collected a vast store of detail about the life of the young people of Ta'u. The six months had made her question some of the beliefs she held as a typical young American woman. Before she went to Samoa, for example, she would not have doubted that it was a good thing to send the village children to school. Now, she saw that education could cause problems.

It was the young girls of six or seven who looked after the babies of the family, while the boys ran errands and saw to many household tasks like lighting fires and cleaning lamps. When the children went to school for most of the day, the households were completely disorganized. With the children there, family life ran like clockwork. Without them, the parents – especially the mothers – couldn't cope.

It was a confused and uncertain Margaret Mead who left Samoa for the journey home. Field work had not turned out quite as she had expected.

Above: Among the Mundugumor, and other New Guinea peoples, the men met in their own ceremonial houses, called House Tamburans, from which women were excluded. Margaret Mead found this society, based on rivalry rather than affection between the sexes, repellent.

Left: Paulo was one of the children of the chief's household where Margaret stayed soon after arriving in Samoa. "I never spent a more peacefully happy and comfortable ten days in my life," she wrote.

17

Like minds

Margaret's voyage was by way of Australia and Europe. She planned to meet her husband Luther Cressman, who had been touring Europe, in France. They were to spend some time together before returning to the United States.

One of the passengers on the voyage from Australia was a young New Zealand psychologist, Reo Fortune. He was on his way to England to take up a scholarship at Cambridge University. The traders and tourists who made up the rest of the passenger-list of the *SS Chitral* were not very interesting to the two young academics. They spent most of their time together striking ideas off each other like matches.

By the time the *SS Chitral* reached Europe, Margaret and Reo had fallen in love.

At first, Margaret seems to have tried to ignore the obvious. In Europe, she meekly allowed Luther to show her the sights and tell her about his year as a tourist. But her thoughts continued to revolve around her months in Samoa. She remembered the intense conversations with Reo during those weeks at sea. Slowly, she realized how different her interests, view of life and depth of experience were from her husband's.

"Coming of Age in Samoa"

Back in New York, Margaret Mead began to write her account of her field work, *Coming of Age in Samoa*. Luther started a new career as a lecturer.

As Margaret wrote her book, she felt more and more uncertain about her future. Her marriage to Luther seemed pointless and empty. Meanwhile, Cambridge University had not worked out well for Reo Fortune and he was planning to do field research in the southern Pacific. On a visit to Reo in Germany in the summer of 1927, Margaret agreed to marry him and join him in New Guinea if they could arrange funds. Then she returned to New York to say goodbye to Luther. "We spent a week together," she wrote, "unmarred by reproaches or feelings of guilt."

There had already been one disappointment for Margaret. To have work published is all-important to an academic researcher. But despite Boas's support, the first draft of *Coming of Age in Samoa* had been turned down by a leading American publisher, Harper. Recovering swiftly from this blow, she sent the draft to another publisher, William Morrow, who was just setting up in business. He agreed to take it if she would add three extra chapters explaining what her findings meant for Americans concerned about "reckless and rebellious youth."

Events were now moving quickly in Margaret's life. Reo had obtained a grant and had already started work in New Guinea. Margaret applied for, and eventually got, a fellowship to fund a year's work there. Her plan was to study very young children. Meanwhile she was devizing and making test materials to use in her work, and arranging her divorce. She also had to write the extra chapters for William Morrow. At last, in the late summer of

The success of Margaret's early field work was due largely to her ability to join with children in their games and everyday activities. She was delighted to find in Manus, New Guinea, that it was "a paradise for children. They have no work except to run errands and that involves paddling in the water." There was plenty of time for them to play and for Margaret to study them. Here, she is decorating their hair with strands of scarlet celluloid ribbon.

One of Margaret
Mead's interests was the
variety of ways in which
different peoples
marked the change
from childhood to
adolescence in initiation
ceremonies. She found
many examples in the
southern Pacific, but
such ceremonies are
world-wide. Above: In
Sierra Leone, Africa,
children's faces are
painted white for the
occasion. Right: The
son of an Indian noble
rides in front of the
people.

1928, Margaret Mead, aged twenty-six, set off on the next chapter of her life.

Coming of Age in Samoa was still with the printers and, in those days before air mail, it was many months before Margaret learned that her book was a best seller. In fact, it was such a success that William Morrow ordered a second printing as soon as the first was published.

Painless adolescence

Coming of Age in Samoa is a detailed study of the sexual and family customs of teenage girls in Samoa (though "teenage" was not a word used in the 1920s). There were also many picturesque descriptions of the ritual songs and dances, costumes and ornaments of the villagers. But there were unavoidable gaps in Margaret's account of life in Samoa. As a woman she was not allowed to attend the all-male meetings where political, religious or economic matters were discussed. So, although she found out about how families worked, she discovered little about the workings of the wider community. Later in her life, this was to bring her criticism.

After the hurricane on Ta'u, all the efforts of the villagers were concentrated on re-building the islanders' ruined homes. Many social ceremonies and rituals that Margaret expected to attend had to be called off. As a result, more of Margaret's information came from the girls she interviewed, than from less formal meetings with villagers.

Margaret Mead had found in Samoa, she wrote, a society where life was casual and easy – "laid back", as we would say today. "The Samoan background, which makes growing up so easy, so simple a matter, is the general casualness of the whole society.... From the first months of life, when the child is handed carelessly from one woman's hands to another's, the lesson is learned of not caring for one person greatly, not setting high hopes on any one relationship." In the United States, personal and family tensions were at their greatest during the teenage years. By contrast, adolescence

"We feel grateful to Miss Mead for having undertaken to identify herself so completely with Samoan youth that she gives us a lucid and clear picture of the joys and difficulties encountered by the young individual in a culture so entirely different from our own.... Much of what we ascribe to human nature is no more than a reaction to the restraints put upon us by our civilization."
Franz Boas, from the foreword to "Coming of Age in Samoa".

"We are accustomed to consider all those actions that are part and parcel of our own culture, standards which we follow automatically, as common to all mankind.... Courtesy, modesty, good manners, conformity to definite ethical standards are universal, but what constitutes courtesy, modesty, good manners, and ethical standards is not universal. It is instructive to know that standards differ in the most unexpected ways. It is still more important to know how the individual reacts to these standards."
Franz Boas, from the foreword to "Coming of Age in Samoa".

Opposite top: The 1920s stereotype of American family life: father – "the breadwinner"– goes off to business, leaving his wife to look after the home and children. When Margaret published her first book, "Coming of Age in Samoa", many Americans were offended by her praise for a very different kind of family life, and her implied criticism of the American way.

Opposite bottom: One of the questions Margaret posed in "Coming of Age in Samoa" was whether Western societies made any real attempt to understand their young people. In the 1920s, more so than today, this was a typical school scene, with bored teenagers confined to their desks and longing for the bell to signal the end of the lesson.

in Samoa was "the age of maximum ease". The teenage years were free of stress and conflict.

The extended family

Margaret put the lack of tension in Samoa down to the system of raising children. This took place in extended families of fifteen or twenty related people. No one had a special claim on a particular child. The child "belonged" to the group, not to its parents. This meant that it was not handicapped, as sometimes happens elsewhere, by having unloving parents, or "spoilt" by parents who were too indulgent. In Samoa, there was always affection to be had from someone in the "easy, friendly warmth" of the extended family.

The ideal of the small family, each member dependent on the others, is dear to the hearts of Americans in particular. It was not surprising that Margaret's praise of the Samoans brought her criticism. But for parents worried about teenage sexual conduct, there was worse to come. The easy, friendly warmth of the extended family spread also, she went on, into the sexual lives of Samoan teenagers. Young Samoans regarded sex as a kind of game whose skills had to be learned and then tried with as many temporary partners as possible. They had no thought of romantic love. Nor did they think of sex as a matter of men "conquering" women. It brought them no conflict with their parents. In the United States, by contrast, teenagers received confusing messages about sex. Their instincts and bodies told them that they were ready to play, but society disapproved of sex before marriage – and marriage was for people in their twenties.

Throwing all this into the United States' worries about the need to control the lives, and especially the sex lives, of rebellious teenagers was like tossing a firework into a gunpowder store. But what one reviewer called "Miss Mead's graphic picture of Polynesian free love" was both appalling and appealing at the same time.

The idea of "free love" – free from ties to one particular partner – was very much talked about in the 1920s, although more people talked about it than actually tried it. But there was a shock at Margaret's apparent approval of a way of life that overthrew what "every decent American" had been taught about sex, love and marriage. Margaret Mead was not, of course, suggesting that all American teenagers should be encouraged to throw themselves into orgies of sex. But some of her critics believed, or pretended to believe, that she was.

There were also some cheap attacks on her private life. What kind of young American woman was this, some newspapers asked, who was married, but insisted on keeping her maiden name? What decent American wife would leave her husband to go and spend six months living with savages?

"An outstanding achievement"

What mattered most to Margaret, though, was the opinion of respected anthropologists. The quality of her field work has been seriously questioned in recent years, but, at the time, *Coming of Age in Samoa* was greeted with wild praise. A leading anthropologist, Bronislaw Malinowski, had warned Margaret before she left for Samoa that she could achieve nothing in such a short time. But he admitted his mistake, and called *Coming of Age in Samoa* an "outstanding achievement."

But perhaps Margaret Mead's greatest triumph was to have brought anthropology out of the lecture-room and into the understanding of the public. *Coming of Age in Samoa* was, and still is, a very readable book. For the first time, ordinary people who were not scholars could see the point of anthropology. Margaret's study of the way family or kinship relationships varied among different peoples gave them new ways of looking at themselves and the people round them.

New Guinea

By the time she read the reviews of her first book, Margaret was at work in New Guinea. In October 1928 she had married Reo Fortune in New Zealand,

may also have been put into her mind by Reo's attitude to her as a woman. Margaret wanted to see how and why the men and women of primitive societies organized their male and female roles. Were some activities and interests "naturally" male and others "naturally" female, or was this decided by custom and tradition? It was the "nature or nurture" question again.

In Arapesh, the split between Margaret and Reo grew wider. She accepted the people, but Reo could not get on with them. He became infuriated with their servant boys and would threaten to hit them. Margaret would have to defend them. "Reo came," she wrote later, "from a culture in which boys were physically disciplined and men beat women, whereas I came from a family tradition within which probably no man had lifted a hand to strike a wife or child for several generations." It was another sign of how far apart they were.

Depressed

But the Arapesh were difficult to talk to, and
Margaret began to feel depressed. It seemed that
the lucky streak that had guided her professional
life so far had run out. Nothing much happened in
Arapesh, and so there was little on which to base
any research. Her second marriage was falling
apart. The hostile review of *Growing Up in New
Guinea* still stung her. The eight months in Arapesh
were one of the low points of her life.

In 1932, they moved on to the Yuat River and
the Mundugumor people. These were "a fierce
group of cannibals who occupied the best high
ground near the riverbank." They had a history of
raiding nearby villages and carrying off the women.
"Reo decided that this time he would do the culture
and I could do the language, the children, and the
technology." But they could find only one person
who had any sound information. The mosquitoes
were frightful. "It was extraordinarily hard and
unrewarding work." And there was not much for
Margaret to involve herself in.

Men and women alike were fierce, possessive,
and rejected any idea of warmth or affection.
Women wanted sons and men wanted daughters,
and newborn babies of the "wrong" sex were
thrown alive into the river. Not surprisingly, Margaret reacted to all this with horror. This increased
when she saw that Reo had some sympathy with
this – to her – revolting culture.

When they left the Yuat River just before Christmas 1932 both Reo and Margaret were despondent.
Their field work had been thin and disappointing.
They needed, they felt, to try again somewhere
else in New Guinea. They had read about the work
of Gregory Bateson, a British anthropologist who
was studying the Iatmul people further along the
New Guinea coast. There was an unwritten rule
that one researcher did not "invade" another's field,
but Margaret and Reo met Gregory Bateson hoping
that he could point them in a new direction.

Bateson took them to the Aimbom Lake. It was
said to be the most beautiful lake in New Guinea.
There were about five hundred Tchambuli people,

living in three small villages. Almost nothing was known about them. They seemed an ideal subject for study.

There could be no greater difference than between the way of life of the Mundugamor and the Tchambuli. The lake-dwellers loved music, art, dancing, acting and putting on festivals. There was always something going on.

This made for an interesting time, but for Margaret there was something even more interesting. The roles of the Tchambuli men and women were the exact opposite of those in American society. It was the women who were the managers, organizers and major workers. Meanwhile, the men devoted much of their time to artistic activities like carving, plaiting, painting and dancing. The men met in their own club-houses to carry on these activities, and the women kept away. It was the women who ran the society, and the men were happy to let them. Margaret wrote that "what the women will think, what the women will say, what the women will do, lies at the back of each man's mind." She did not need to point out the difference in the United States. Her readers knew that there it was the women who worried about what the men would think and do.

Margaret Mead with her third husband, Gregory Bateson. With him, she wrote, she found "the perfect intellectual and emotional working partnership in which there was no pulling and hauling from competing temperamental views of the world" – as there had been with her second husband, Reo Fortune.

Margaret and Reo part

While Reo and Margaret stayed with the Tchambuli, Gregory Bateson was working in a nearby village. The three spent a lot of time together. Gregory had been in the area for a year and a half, and knew the language well. Margaret was glad to use him as a sounding-board for her ideas. Gradually, she found that she was turning to him more often than to her husband Reo. The discussions of the three strayed away from the subject of Margaret's work – masculine and feminine roles and temperaments – to their own temperaments. "By then," Margaret wrote later, "Gregory and I had already established a kind of communication in which Reo did not share."

It was as it had been with Margaret, Luther and

Contrasting styles of male peacockry from opposite sides of the world: above left, a punk in a London street; right, a New Guinea man in a head-dress of birds' feathers.

Reo five years before. A more interesting and sympathetic new man was shutting the old one out. When the three left New Guinea in the spring of 1933, they went their separate ways. Margaret sailed for New York, Reo for New Zealand and Gregory for England. But it was clear that Margaret's second marriage was over, and that her third would be to Gregory.

Traditional sex roles

The field work among the Arapesh, the Munduga-mor and the Tchambuli was the basis of Margaret's third book, *Sex and Temperament in Three Primitive Societies*, published in 1935.

By now, people expected a Margaret Mead book to contain challenging ideas. They were not disappointed. The idea that men and women need not necessarily adopt the roles given to them in Western society delighted feminists. The traditional female role as mother, Margaret wrote, was "wasteful of the gifts of many women who could exercise other functions far better than their ability to bear children in an already overpopulated world." The traditional male role was "wasteful of the gifts of many men who could exercise their special personality gifts far better in the home than in the marketplace." Margaret was again raising questions about the accepted pattern of American society where men were breadwinners and women home-makers, and many Americans were resentful.

Blue eyes or brown

Margaret asked whether classifying people by their sex made any more sense than to classify them by, say, whether their eyes were brown or blue. Society might just as easily decide that, for example, all blue-eyed people were "gentle home-makers" and all brown-eyed people were "strong breadwinners." But that way, some people would be forced into roles to which they were not suited. In the same way, Margaret suggested, men and women in Western society, whose temperaments did not make them behave in the ways expected of them, were forced into roles in which they did not fit.

Some readers misunderstood what Margaret was saying. Just as they had thought that her first book was suggesting that American young people should copy the sexual habits of young Samoans, they now thought that she was denying any differences between the sexes.

This was missing the point. Her job as an anthropologist was to report on how different peoples organized their societies and to ask if there was anything that could be learned from her findings. She was not suggesting that there was no difference between men and women. She was merely questioning whether there was good reasoning behind the roles Western society found for them. It was only thirty years after the publication of *Sex and Temperament* that the idea of "man the breadwinner" and "woman the home-maker" was seriously challenged in the United States – but it was Margaret Mead who had first posed the question.

"Field work is a very difficult thing to do. To do it well, one has to sweep one's mind clear of every presupposition, even those about other cultures in the same part of the world in which one is working.... In the field one can take nothing for granted."
Margaret Mead,
from her autobiography,
"Blackberry Winter".

Processions were part of the rich cultural life that Margaret Mead and Gregory Bateson found in Bali, which she always regarded as the high point of her career in field work. This procession is on its way to a feast by the sea, where the Balinese gods were taken in miniature sedan chairs, protected by ceremonial umbrellas. The feast ended with traditional dancing.

When she wrote the book, Margaret was well aware that the questions she was asking were relevant to her own personal life. When she had been engaged to Luther Cressman, she had planned to have a large family of as many as six children. Medical problems had, she thought, put an end to that dream. She had kept her interest in children and was never happier than when working with them. But, as she wrote later, "my own interest in children did not fit the stereotype of the American career woman or, for that matter, the stereotype of the possessive, managing American wife and mother."

This was what worried some of her critics. They did not know what to make of her. Perhaps she did not know what to make of herself.

Divorce, and a third marriage

Margaret and Reo were divorced in July 1935. Margaret, in New York, and Gregory Bateson, in Cambridge, began to plan a field trip that they could take together as husband and wife. They chose Bali, one of the string of islands in the Indian Ocean that make up what is now Indonesia. It was then a Dutch colony.

This was to be a very different trip from their earlier ones. Bali was a land of over one million people who spoke the same language, compared with a few hundred in the New Guinea cultures they had studied.

Balinese art and culture were already well-known in the United States. There were large numbers of Europeans and Americans living on the island, some of whom had decided to spend the rest of their lives there. There were artists, dancers, musicians, writers and people who were there to observe and enjoy Balinese arts. There would be none of the isolation of previous field trips. And there would be no hurry. Margaret and Gregory planned to stay in Bali for two years.

They were married in Singapore on March 13, 1936 and went on to Bali on a slow boat that pottered from island to island. This was the best-equipped field trip that Margaret had ever taken.

It was the first time that she had used movie film. She and Gregory had the latest cameras and their own developing and printing equipment. Gregory's photography was of a professional standard. They had no recording equipment of their own, but a musician who was on the island studying Balinese music had some, and they used his.

Bali

They arrived in Bali at the end of April. For Margaret, Bali was magic. "What a paradise Bali was for us," she wrote. "Ceremonies every day – if not in this village, then in another only a short distance

A girl's first menstruation – which happened at a later age than in the West – was the occasion for a ceremony in Bali. The two and a half years that Margaret spent in Bali was especially valuable as it gave her time to trace the rituals of puberty, courtship and marriage within the same families.

away. Informants, scribes, secretaries were ready to be trained for the asking. Household help too, and when we came home at midnight dinner would be waiting, hot and delicious.... And every group – the people walking on the roads, or sitting behind the little roadside stalls in which refreshments were sold, or standing, close packed, listening to music – all of them were rewarding to the photographer."

The richness of the Balinese culture astonished and delighted them. There were shadow plays featuring puppets shadowed against a thin screen under a swinging light. There were trance dances, in which girl performers danced like robots. There

were traditional costumes and marks, orchestral concerts, Balinese operas, great feasts.

"We responded to it," wrote Margaret, "by working at fever pitch." The results of the two years in Bali included no fewer than twenty-eight thousand photographs, collections of paintings, carvings, children's drawings and shadow-play puppets and countless reels of movie film. Most valuable of all, Margaret and Gregory worked out a system of reference and cross-indexing that could identify where each item came from, who was singing or dancing, and the names of the people in the background or the instruments that were being played.

"We were never again, after the silence of our first day [on Bali], out of the sound of music, if it was only the tinkle of the bells that the women fastened to their knives or the flute played by some lonely peasant watching over his crops in a far field."
Margaret Mead,
from her autobiography,
"Blackberry Winter".

"Here in a mountain village Mead also had the first and only real home she was ever to have, a house built of pavilions joined by covered walks and furniture made by Balinese craftsmen. After the rigours of New Guinea everything seemed to be accomplished with miraculous ease. At night it was romantically lit by tiny glass lamps."
Phyllis Grosskurth, from
"Margaret Mead. A Life
of Controversy".

The clouds of war

From Bali, Margaret and Gregory returned to New Guinea for a year. But it seems likely that Margaret had found in Bali the place where she wanted to live for the rest of her life. Before they left in March 1938, she and Gregory made plans for an ambitious expedition. It would cover a number of the sciences that collected under the "umbrella" of anthropology. There would be an educational organization to teach members of the expedition Balinese language and culture. They even chose the building for the headquarters and rented it for three years.

By now it was 1939. Hitler's armies were on the march in Europe. It was clear that another world war was not far away. On the ship that took Margaret and Gregory home, British passengers were talking about being called up to fight. Gregory, who was British, felt that it was his duty to return to Britain if war broke out. Although it was to be two years before the United States came into World War II, many people – including Margaret – felt that once war started it would engulf the world.

It was no time to be planning further field trips or setting up a field headquarters in Bali. As it turned out, this was just as well. During World War II, Bali was occupied by Japanese troops. If Margaret and Gregory had been there, they would certainly have been sent to a prison camp.

The direct result of the Bali field trip was *Balinese Character,* produced jointly with Gregory and illustrated with over seven hundred of the twenty-five thousand photographs they had taken in Bali. It was intended not only as a record of their field trip, but also as a model of how research findings in the field could be presented. They also put together four twenty-minute films on aspects of life in Bali.

Margaret has a baby

Meanwhile, Margaret had something else to think about. She was pregnant. Fifteen years before she had been told that she could never have a child. Since then, she had had a number of miscarriages. Now, she was overjoyed.

She was thirty-eight, an age when the birth of a first child was likely to be difficult if not dangerous. She was advised to take things easy.

Margaret Mead had by now been a student of child development for most of her adult life. On her field trips she had seen the birth of many babies. Yet she found that she was just as prone as any first-time mother to worries about her child. She checked her family's history for health problems. She remembered that some of her relatives were prone to deafness. "There also were members of my family," she recalled, "whom I did not find attractive or endearing, and I knew my child might take after them." This was the "nature or nurture" argument brought home in the closest possible way! Yet, she saw the forthcoming birth as an interesting event from the professional as well as the personal point of view. She even went as far as arranging for a friend to film it, and "slowing down" the birth so that the friend could fit a new flashbulb.

Mary Catherine Bateson, known to the family as Cathy, was born on December 8, 1939, three months after World War II had broken out. "Bringing up Cathy," Margaret wrote, "was an intellectual as well as an emotionally exciting adventure." It

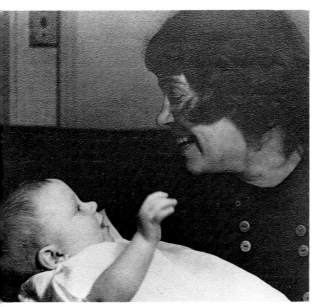

Margaret with her daughter Catherine, then a few weeks old. The birth of Catherine gave Margaret a new insight into women's lives. She resisted fashionable views (encouraged by male doctors) about childbirth and the care of the young child, insisting on a natural birth and on ignoring the current fads about babies' feeding times.

was an opportunity for her to put into practice her ideas from years of observation of parents and children. But she knew that there was a danger in this. It was that Cathy would be seen more as a live piece of field work than as a child of loving parents.

Although Margaret had by now a world-wide reputation as an anthropologist, neither she nor Gregory had had the chance to save any money. Before Cathy was born, Margaret had done some occasional lecturing. She now returned to this, together with part-time work at the American Museum of Natural History, to earn their keep and pay for a nanny.

When the United States entered the war in 1941, there was plenty of work for experts who had studied the problems of change in people's lives. For Americans joining the forces, for the wives and children left at home, and for women drafted into war work, World War II was the biggest change that could be imagined. Both Margaret and Gregory were in demand for ideas on helping people cope with the problems of separation and new

Margaret Mead studies an exhibit at the American Museum of Natural History, where she held a series of appointments from 1926 until her death in 1978. She was well aware that, but for the reputation she had built up in the early years of her career, she would have been "frozen out" of the museum once she became a mother – as happened to so many other talented women of her generation.

experiences. But this was not anthropological field work, which Margaret felt to be the core of her life. And while the war went on there was no chance of returning to the southern Pacific.

Into the field again

It was June 1953 before Margaret felt free to return to her first love, field work. By now, she was divorced from Gregory and Cathy was thirteen.

There had been great upheavals in the southern Pacific since 1939. Great movements of thousands of Japanese and American troops through the southern Pacific had changed the way of life in the islands for ever. It had also changed the ideas of many of the people.

Most of the islands were still under the control of European countries, Australia or the United States. After the war ended, independence movements sprang up. Their aim was to free the islands from colonial rule. There were protests, strikes, and sometimes open warfare and terrorism. In 1949, the Dutch government gave independence to the string of islands that made up Indonesia. Bali was free.

These events had altered the character of the places Margaret had known well in the 1930s. Another change was for the better. Since the 1930s new equipment had been developed which helped the field worker. There were portable electric generators, new photographic lighting – and, most valuable of all, the portable tape recorder. It was no longer necessary, as it had been in Bali before World War II, to use cumbersome equipment with poor quality sound and limited recording time. Cameras, too, had improved.

So although field work in the 1950s might be more difficult in some ways, at least it could be done with better equipment. Added to this was the advantage of the increased ease and speed of travel. It was important to Margaret, with a young daughter to think about, that a journey that would have taken two months twenty years before, now took only two days.

"Mead was thoroughly at home in New York. She had her secure job at the Museum of Natural History, a wide network of supportive friends, and the status of a national celebrity. Bateson was just as hungry for recognition as his wife, but there was no way he could compete with her. 'It was almost a principle of pure energy,' he recalled ruefully. 'I couldn't keep up and she couldn't stop.'"
Phyllis Grosskurth, from "Margaret Mead. A Life of Controversy".

"In these years her appearance became more and more schoolmarmish – something the American public seemed to like. What mattered most to her was energy, and the house was bursting with noise – people constantly coming and going, and talk over the table long after dinner was finished."
Phyllis Grosskurth, from "Margaret Mead. A Life of Controversy".

41

A sand painting from New Guinea. As a result of the work of Margaret Mead and other collectors, the bold lines and vibrant style of the art of the southern Pacific islands has become an important influence on Western art. But the production of works of art as souvenirs for tourists debased the originals.

The world in a saucer

For her first post-war trip, Margaret Mead, aged fifty-one, chose to return to Peri village on Manus in the Admiralty Islands, which she had last seen in 1929. She was interested in the changes that had taken place within a generation, and wanted to find out how the villagers had reacted to them.

But Margaret was soon to realize that changes in Manus went far beyond anything she could have imagined on her earlier trip.

In the Peri of the 1920s, the people had had no knowledge of anything outside their own villages. Their picture of the world was "as a giant saucer, with the waters of the sea sloping up and away on every side." The passage of time was marked by the monthly flow of water over the reef which brought them the fish which was their livelihood. They knew nothing of their history except for stories of things that had happened in their parents' or their grandparents' time.

The changes had started soon after Margaret left Manus in 1929. When she was there, Manus had not heard of Christianity. Within a short time, though, Roman Catholic missionaries arrived and converted the Manus people. This brought them some basic education, but the mission schools mainly taught Bible stories.

During World War II Manus and the rest of the Admiralty Islands had been occupied by the Japanese. In 1946, American forces landed and recaptured them. After a period of American occupation, the islands were returned to Australian control.

This rapid chain of events would have had huge effects even on the most advanced countries. To the people of the small island of Manus, it seemed that their world had been turned upside down two or three times.

Manus had been for a time a base for transporting troops to and from the Far East. Margaret estimated that over a million white men had passed through the island. This was an astonishing experience for a primitive people.

Above and left: Margaret recorded the traditional culture of New Guinea only just in time. In the 1930s, Roman Catholic missionaries arrived and traditional stories were replaced with stories from the Bible. After World War II, Western-style education followed. "The whole thing is fascinating, a little heartbreaking," Margaret wrote. Although medical care and schools were welcome and much needed, she felt that Western ideas had been imported to the islands without enough thought about the impact they would have on people whose culture had not changed for hundreds of years.

"Which is harder for them to assimilate and understand – a savage way of life, which in so many respects is like that of their grandfathers, now so enthusiastically abandoned, or a way of life which belongs to the modern world, the world of planes that fly overhead and news that comes over the radio?"

Margaret Mead, writing from Peri in 1965, from "Letters from the Field".

Wonder and envy

And the people of Manus looked with wonder not only at the soldiers, but at their equipment: aircraft, bulldozers, searchlights, torpedo boats. The young people looked with envy as well as wonder. They saw how a bulldozer with one driver could do as much work in a day as a team of Manus men using hand tools in months. They enjoyed the canned food and other goods which were showered upon them by American forces – delightful things for which it was not necessary to work!

The young people talked among themselves. When the time came, they would make changes. No more back-breaking work with hand tools. No more old-fashioned ceremonies organized by the old men of the villages, locked into the poor and hopeless past.

The Americans went, leaving behind stores of canned food and other things which were immensely valuable to villagers who had lived all their lives on the edge of poverty. Corrugated iron, plywood, metal shelving, canvas sheeting, chairs, tables, paraffin lamps – the list of dumped items was endless. Inevitably, these stocks ran low, and there were no more where they had come from....

But wait a minute. Where *had* they come from?

Changes on Manus

Before the 1940s, civilization in many of the islands had not advanced much beyond the Stone Age, but the upheavals of World War II had exposed many more communities to Western goods and equipment. Suddenly, without warning and for no reason that the islanders could see, several thousands of years of civilization had arrived at once. The white people's aircraft brought things that the islanders had never seen, or heard of, or even dreamed of. Then, just as suddenly, the white people's aircraft had gone.

When Margaret Mead re-visited Manus in 1953, the local people now wore Western clothes. In Peri, the houses over the lagoon had been demolished and new houses, with European-style kitchens and windows, built on shore, although still on stilts. Scrap drums left behind by the Americans were used to store water. New villages had been built and each one had a central square, which served as a meeting place, and a council with an elected leader. There were plans – but only plans, because there was no money to turn them into realities – for hospitals, clinics, schools and banks.

All this had happened after the end of the war when there was no one like Margaret Mead around to observe it. As a result no one knows exactly what had happened. By observing and talking to the local people, Margaret tried to piece together the story.

During the American occupation, she thought, the islands had seen a different kind of society at work. "They were caught up in the spectacle of so many people all alike, the great scale of the army barracks, the bulldozer constructions, and the great planes." They added to this envy of American technology an admiration of the way Americans behaved. "They contrasted their own endless quarrelling over a single broken clay pot and the American willingness to spend any amount of money, time and equipment to save the life of

Margaret's return visit to Manus in 1953 provided a sharp illustration of the changes that had come with Western influence during World War II. The group at the bottom was photographed in 1928. Second from the right is John Kilipak, then a thirteen-year-old cookboy. Below: Kilipak in 1953.

a single soldier." They also noticed that black American troops were dressed, housed and paid as well as the white people. "They felt that the Americans had made the 'men of Africa all right.'"

Progress, but ...

But underlying the apparent success, there was a note of sadness. The achievements so far had been made by using dumped American material. This had been used up by 1953. And Margaret Mead felt that the Manus people were racing ahead of themselves.

"Their imaginative grasp of the possibilities of modernity," she reported, "outruns their resources. They understand how to tell time and set a meeting for 'one o'clock'. But there are only two clocks and one watch in the village and the meeting is less likely to start on time than when meetings were set by the sun. They have learned about dates, but they have no calendar, so what day it is is a matter for protracted discussion – or was until I arrived. They want good materials and good equipment, but they cannot write to order it nor have they any way of sending money."

An anthropologist is a reporter. It was not for Margaret Mead to judge whether the changes she had seen on Manus were a good or bad thing, though she had – like many people – a sentimental regret for the vanished past. Most of the adults she spoke to on Manus in 1953 had been children when she was there in 1929. They had grown up in a world of superstition, fear and poverty.

It was easy for someone from New York to say that trying to build a future out of American scrap was a hopeless task. But the Manus people were doing their best with what – as it must have seemed to them – luck or the gods had thrown their way. And they were excited about it. They wanted everything to happen all at once. Margaret's verdict was that, in trying to cope with social changes in the Pacific, the West wanted to go too slowly. It also wanted to choose "which bits of our social pattern to pass on." But in Manus "a backward people,

"And in her flowing cape and with the forked cherrywood stick that [Margaret Mead] now carried with her everywhere, she spoke and looked like a prophet, a role she found particularly satisfying. Americans liked her for being fat and plain. People frequently told her that she reminded them of their mothers."

Phyllis Grosskurth, from "Margaret Mead. A Life of Controversy".

46

"What is there for young anthropologists to do? In one sense, everything. The best possible work has not yet been done. If I were twenty-one today I would elect to join the communicating network of those young people, the world over, who recognize the urgency of life-supporting change – as an anthropologist."

Margaret Mead,
from her autobiography,
"Blackberry Winter".

making the choices themselves, picked a whole pattern, each detail of which they think is right."

Margaret's return trip to Manus marked a change in her professional interests. Previously, she had been interested mainly in the slow and natural changes that happened in communities. In Manus, she was faced with the result of huge changes that had happened suddenly because of the war. These in turn had led to further changes from inside. From 1953 on, she became more interested and active in helping the Western world to understand the need for change in under-developed countries like Papua New Guinea and how money and technical aid could best be used.

Winding down

The return to Manus was the last field trip on which Margaret did most of the work herself. She was now over fifty. Even with the conveniences of modern travel, conditions in remote places were harsh and challenging. She had also to think of launching her daughter, Cathy, into the world. She satisfied her thirst for field work by regular correspondence with friends and students who were working in the same territory, though often with other interests. Over the years she had built up a network of contacts in a wide variety of work such as psychology, child development, education and various branches of medicine.

In 1960, Catherine – as she chose to call herself now she was adult – married. Margaret now felt more free to enjoy herself. Between 1964 and 1975 she made a series of flying visits to field workers who were members of her network. She was also writing and editing a steady stream of books, held a number of part-time academic posts, and was in demand as a speaker at national and international conferences.

The flying visits were often trips "down Memory Lane." This was so when she went back again to Manus in 1964 and again met Lokus. Lokus had been a "houseboy" in the house where she and Reo had lived in 1928. When she went back in 1953,

In 1954, Margaret revisited the Manus village of Peri, where she had worked in 1928. She admired the new school and the way it had "opened the doors to the world" for the Manus children, but she worried that education would tempt young people to move away, leaving only the old and sick in the village.

he had been cook in the house of friend. Now, aged fifty or so, he was chief cook and in charge of a household. He seemed like an old man with failing sight and hearing. But he remembered small details of her first visit. "Every event," she wrote home, "is tied firmly into the shared past."

In the eleven years since her last visit, progress had made another great leap forward. Over thirty Manus children had gone on to some form of higher education outside the village, as students, teachers or nurses. "The new education has opened the doors to the world," Margaret wrote, but it also had a sad side. The Manus were happy for boys to go away for training, but girls who had been away and come back were treated as "damaged goods". No one wanted to marry them. It was not thought right for girls to go among strangers.

Democracy had progressed, and Papua New Guinea now had an elected parliament, though at that time the territory was still administered by Australia. Full independence was granted in 1975.

The thirst for education had resulted in a steady flow of young men, and a lesser one of young women, from Manus. "If the young men go away, who will care for the old?" Margaret asked. She quoted the sad case of one young man who had gone as a student to Australia, had done well, and had returned to Peri in triumph. Then he had received a message calling him to Port Moresby for interview. "This can only mean some new scholarship or opportunity," Margaret wrote. "But it is hard for his father, with his family of children all excelling in school, and for his uncle, who has prepared such a perfect room for him, to understand."

Voices of opposition

Margaret Mead's books – especially the early, challenging, best-selling ones – had made her famous. She was listened to and respected by everyone whose work touched her own, such as teachers, specialists in child care and development, sociologists, psychologists and many more. But her books were also read with interest by ordinary readers. They were fascinated to compare the way people related to each other in Samoa or New Guinea with their own experience of family and community life.

Since Margaret did her early work, films produced by anthropologists – especially those shown on television – have made studies of faraway peoples familiar. But in *Coming of Age in Samoa* and *Growing Up in New Guinea*, Margaret Mead showed the ordinary reader, for the first time, what it was like to live in a society without technology or modern understanding of the world.

From the beginning, Margaret had her critics. First, there were those who opposed her in the "nature or nurture" argument. They were not particularly worrying. In the academic world, there is always a good deal of argument, often greatly enjoyed by both sides. Argument is one of the ways in which ideas are filtered, looked at upside down, refined and then moved forward.

More damaging was the coverage of her work

51

Pago Pago, in American Samoa, saw the first contact between Samoans and Western ideas when it had become an American naval base before World War I. By the time Margaret Mead arrived in 1925, the native economy and culture were already being debased, with market traders pitching their sales at the tourists. By now, the goods like those in the picture have very little in common with the early culture of the people.

in the press. What she had written in *Coming of Age in Samoa,* for example, was so simplified for newspaper readers that it became completely distorted and was turned into political ammunition. One sneering newspaper cartoon at the time of a United States' presidential election, for example, showed her as a candidate, with a human skull strung around her neck as an ornament.

Questions about Samoa

With the election of Franklin Roosevelt as president in 1932, there was a new mood in the United States. Schemes for full employment, social security and better education – known collectively as the New Deal – were set up. The atmosphere was one in which new ideas flourished and were welcomed, Margaret Mead's included.

After World War II, the mood had changed. As individuals and as a nation, Americans were terrified of the spread of Communism. Liberal thinkers, actors, film directors, writers and academics like Margaret Mead came – quite unjustly – under suspicion of wanting to attack the American way of life. It may have been partly this that led her, after 1953, to spend time in the field again, away from the storms of politics at home.

But a bigger storm was brewing. It involved a New Zealand anthropologist, Derek Freeman, who had been researching in Western Samoa since 1940. At first a follower of Margaret Mead and the "nurture" school of thought, he gradually came to question her findings and her methods of research.

The area of his own research was different from hers, but he was assured by Samoans that there was no major difference in the way of life in the two halves of the group of islands. By the time he left Samoa in November 1943, he wrote, he knew that he would one day have to question publicly the picture of Samoan life that Margaret Mead had presented.

In 1964, Derek Freeman met Margaret and, in a long private conversation, told her of his views. This was the start of a long correspondence over the next ten years. He was not the only critic of Margaret's picture of Samoa. In the 1970s, she met Samoan university students in the United States and Australia who asked her to revise her Samoa book. She refused, writing (in the preface to a new edition) that *Coming of Age in Samoa* was "true to what I saw in Samoa and what I was able to convey of what I saw, true to the state of our knowledge of human behavior as it was in the mid-1920s." Asking her to revise her impressions fifty years later was rather like asking someone who had taken a photograph of a village in 1925 to re-touch it in the 1970s to include houses that had been built since.

By 1978, Derek Freeman had finished a draft of his book, which he offered to send to Margaret for comment. She did not reply, and a few months later, on November 15, she died, a month before her seventy-seventh birthday. It is doubtful whether, if she had had the opportunity, she would have

"I have resolved the way in which I have been publicly discussed, lambasted and lampooned.... I have taken the stand, in my own mind and in replying to others, that I have no right to resent the public expression of attitudes that I arouse in those whom I do not know and who know me only through what I have written or said and through the words that the mass media, correctly or incorrectly, have attributed to me."

Margaret Mead,
from her autobiography,
"Blackberry Winter".

taken up the challenge. She was living a peaceful old age with her grandchildren around her, and she had, in any case, never enjoyed the cut and thrust of academic argument. But we will never know how she would have defended herself against the serious criticisms that Derek Freeman made.

Was Margaret Mead right?

The book, *Margaret Mead and Samoa*, was published in the United States in 1983. It caused an immediate sensation.

Coming of Age in Samoa was, and still is, the best-selling anthropological book of all time. Generations of students – including Derek Freeman himself – had been taught to see it as a model of anthropological research. But according to him it was hollow.

Margaret had spent only ten weeks learning the Samoan language, as she had admitted. This meant, Derek Freeman said, that she could have had only a smattering when she began to interview her sample of Samoan girls. She had chosen to live in the household of a United States Navy family, the Holts. This, according to Freeman, would have identified her as part of the naval government which many Samoans both feared and resented. Instead of interviewing the Samoan girls in their homes in their own villages, they were called to the European-style Navy house.

Not a paradise on earth

For these reasons and others, Derek Freeman argued that Margaret had never found out the true situation in Samoa. It was far from being the paradise on earth that she had described, where there was no hatred or tension and where the happy natives lived only to love. Samoa was a violent society. As for "free love", Samoans kept to and if necessary enforced a code of sexual conduct which was as strict in the most restrictive American communities. It was the picture of themselves as sexually casual that had upset the Samoans most.

"I have yet to meet a Samoan who agrees with Mead's assertion that adolescence in Samoan society is smooth, untroubled and unstressed.... Adolescents would tell us of the tensions between themselves and their parents, and of their emotional distress during altercations with their families or when they were heavily dominated by someone in authority.",
Derek Freeman, from "Margaret Mead and Samoa".

54

Freeman suggested that Margaret's Samoan informants had teased her with stories about "casual love under the palm trees." He pointed out that Margaret, aged twenty-three and slight in stature, was smaller than some of the girls she was interviewing and that, as she wrote, they treated her as "one of themselves." Freeman did not go on to suggest this, but it is possible that since she was of an age with them – and they had no way of knowing how old she was – they were merely boasting about their sex lives in the way teenage girls and boys do. They may have let their imaginations make up for what they lacked in real experience.

Freeman's conclusion was that Margaret's work on Samoa was accepted uncritically by Franz Boas, Ruth Benedict and their colleagues because it agreed with their own theories.

Fact or fiction?

Nothing in Margaret's later work attracted such detailed criticism, but Derek Freeman's book put a question-mark over the whole of her career. There is now no way of knowing whether what she reported from Samoa in 1925 was "the truth". In a way it hardly matters. Anthropology is not a science of facts.

A chemist knows that if you expose a piece of iron to moist air, a layer of iron oxide, or rust, will form on the surface of the iron. It always happens like that, and it is always iron oxide, not some other chemical compound, that forms. But anthropology is concerned with observing the patterns of how human beings behave. They don't always behave in the same way – and they don't always observe in the same way.

We all know this from our own experience. If you hear someone describing what happened on an occasion when you were also present, you will notice differences between their description and what you saw. Two people describing a television show, for example, will often choose to highlight different parts of it.

It may be quite true that Margaret Mead got

"We are thus confronted in the case of Margaret Mead's Samoan researches with an instructive example of how, as evidence is sought to substantiate a cherished doctrine, the deeply held beliefs of those involved may lead them unwittingly into error."
    Derek Freeman, from "Margaret Mead and Samoa".

> *"There is hope, I believe, in seeing the human adventure as a whole and in the shared trust that knowledge about mankind, sought in reverence for life, can bring life."*
>
> Margaret Mead,
> from her autobiography,
> "Blackberry Winter".

56

some things wrong. We can only trust her word that *Coming of Age in Samoa* is a record of what she saw. But even if the picture she gave of Samoa in the 1920s is faulty, the book is still valuable in other ways. It shows in detail how field work was done at that time. It shows how families and communities in a society far away from modern influences organized themselves. And Margaret wrote about the way humans behave in a manner that gave us a vocabulary for understanding our own families and communities.

Out of the museum

Anthropology began in the nineteenth century. Exploration and settlement in other parts of the world had shown to Western civilizations the wide variety of patterns of character and ways of behaving among the earth's inhabitants. Anthropology was concerned with how different races and groups adapted to their environments, how they pictured the whole world, and how their language and their arts – that is, their culture – reflected their ideas.

Until early in this century only a few people

Above and opposite: Weddings are not merely picturesque ceremonies, but the focus of cultural beliefs about the nature and role of the family. The differing detail of these three weddings tells us something about their cultural background. One of Margaret Mead's contributions to the understanding of other cultures was to look for the meaning behind feasts, festivals and ceremonies.

knew of the discoveries and theories of anthropologists and had seen the examples of different arts and crafts that they had collected in the field. They were locked up in museum cabinets and filed away in academic papers and notebooks.

Nineteenth century anthropologists tended to treat people they were studying as "specimens", as if they were butterflies or fish. It was as if the people themselves had no contribution to make. They were observed and notes were made on them using the eyes of nineteenth century Westerners. Little attempt was made to get inside their minds or to try to see their point of view.

Margaret Mead combined the academic approach with a more human view of research. She drew up enormous tables of kinship showing the relationships of the villagers she studied, and kept detailed records of the important events in their lives. But she also treated the villagers as individual personalities with their own stories to tell. She was intensely interested in and sympathetic with people as human beings, not merely as objects to study. This gave her writing a vitality which appealed to the reader who was not a specialist.

She brought anthropology out of the museum drawer and the filing cabinet and made an understanding of the outlines of the subject available to everyone.

Opening up the world

Margaret Mead did not invent such terms as *kinship groups, the extended family, taboos,* and other anthropological expressions that are in common use today. But the fact that they are so widely used and understood is due mainly to her writing, and in particular to her earlier books. And by reading her accounts of everyday life in primitive cultures we can see how to interpret the way people relate to one another. Margaret Mead tells us what things they think are important and how they react to major life experiences such as marriage, the birth of children and death.

In a letter from the field in 1967, Margaret wrote:

"It is only through this kind of intense living in face-to-face relationships that the life and culture of a whole people can be fully experienced. It is through the records of such closely bound lives that we may hope to understand the human need for continuity, repetitive experience and intimacy. For intimacy has its source in just these familiar repetitions of laughter at old jokes, remembered anger at old quarrels, meals eaten together in the same twilight and children listening to accounts of things that happened before their parents were born, stories told and retold."

Margaret Mead's gift

In Western culture, with its many diversions, we know how true this is. This kind of intimacy is at the heart of family festivals such as Christmas. It was Margaret Mead's gift that she could take us into the heart of family festivals on the other side of the world, festivals of people who knew nothing of the world but their own village and of whom, without her, we should have known nothing.

Another important aspect of Margaret Mead's work is highlighted by her experiences on her later trips to Peri, where she was able to observe change over three generations. The upheavals caused in Manus by World War II have been mirrored in most countries. Her observations and comments, which were unpopular at the time with many government officials, are relevant to the problems of any under-developed country trying to take its place in the modern world. They raise such questions as: How fast should we go? How much of the old culture should we cling to to give us stability? Which is more important, agriculture or industry, education or medicine? And, most important of all, what will progress do to our people?

Margaret Mead's last visit to Peri was in 1975, the year that Papua New Guinea became an independent nation within the British Commonwealth. On that visit, she was photographed with the widow of the man who had acted as her interpreter forty-seven years before.

The everlasting argument

So, back to the beginning: nature or nurture? It's hard now to imagine how, at the beginning of this century, academics opposed each other so strongly

Alongside language, dance and song, artefacts help to make up a society's image of itself. From her field trips, Margaret brought back a rich variety of artefacts, some gifts specially made for her, others bought after prolonged bargaining. "These people," she had written from Peri in 1929, "love trade better than they love anything in the world."

"Realizing that our own ways are not humanly inevitable nor God-ordained, but are the fruit of a long and turbulent history, we may well examine in turn all of our institutions, thrown into strong relief against the history of other civilizations, and weighing them in the balance, be not afraid to find them wanting."

Margaret Mead, from "Coming of Age in Samoa".

over this argument. The answer to the puzzle may be that the study of heredity in human beings – how characteristics are passed on from parents to children – was then new and seemed to offer a tidy solution to many questions. It is now generally agreed among scientists that the way an individual person behaves is partly inherited and comes partly from what the child learns as he or she grows up. It may be that further research into DNA, the "carrier" of heredity in the cells that make up the body, will reveal more about "nature". In time, the bank of knowledge from anthropological field work may reveal more about patterns of culture.

Every scientist knows that it is dangerous to think that the final answer has been found. In anthropology, as in other disciplines, there is still more to be discovered. Margaret Mead was one of those who have pointed anthropologists along the right road.

Important Dates

1901   Dec 16: Margaret Mead is born.

1918   Margaret graduates from high school and meets Luther Cressman, her first husband.

1919   Margaret begins studies at DePauw College in Indiana State, but leaves after one year.

1920   Margaret goes to Barnard College, Columbia University, New York.

1923   Margaret gains her master's degree in psychology and chooses anthropology for her doctorate.
Sept: Margaret Mead marries Luther Cressman.

1925   Aug: Margaret arrives in Samoa.

1926   Margaret meets Reo Fortune on her voyage back from Samoa to Europe, where she spends the summer with Luther. She returns to New York to write *Coming of Age in Samoa* and starts work as Assistant Curator of Ethnology at the American Museum of Natural History in New York.

1927   Margaret and Reo meet in Germany and decide to marry.

1928   Oct: Margaret Mead and Reo Fortune are married in New Zealand and travel on to Manus, the largest of the Admiralty Islands. *Coming of Age in Samoa* is published.

1929   Margaret returns to New York and writes *Growing Up in New Guinea*.

1930   Margaret starts field work with Reo among the Omaha Indians.

1931   Sept: Margaret and Reo set out for New Guinea and start their field work among the Arapesh.
Sept: Margaret and Reo move on to the Mundugumor.
Dec: Margaret meets Gregory Bateson for the first time.

1933   Feb: Margaret and Reo start their field work among the Tchambuli. When they leave New Guinea, Margaret and Reo separate. She returns to New York and writes *Sex and Temperament in Three Primitive Societies*.

1935   July: Reo and Margaret are divorced. She and Gregory Bateson plan a field trip to Bali.

1936   Mar 13: Margaret and Gregory are married in Singapore and go on to Bali.

1938   Margaret and Gregory do eight months' field work in Iatmul, New Guinea.

1939   Margaret and Gregory return to New York. Margaret becomes pregnant. World War II begins and continues until 1945. Margaret and Gregory start writing *Balinese Character*.
Dec 8: A daughter, Catherine, is born.

1941   Margaret is invited to go to Washington for government war-time work.

1942   *Balinese Character* is published.

1943   Margaret goes to England for a lecture tour.

1952   Margaret goes to Australia for a lecture tour.

1953   Margaret returns to Manus and stays until December.

1954 In addition to her work at the American Museum of Natural History, Margaret is appointed Adjunct Professor of Anthropology at Columbia University.

1957 Margaret makes a second field trip to Bali.

1964 Margaret makes a return visit to Manus.

1966 Margaret makes a field trip to Montserrat, West Indies.

1967 Margaret returns to Tambunam, New Guinea.

1972 Margaret's autobiography, *Blackberry Winter,* is published.

1975 Margaret makes a further visit to Manus.

1978 Nov 15: Margaret Mead, aged seventy-six, dies.

Further Reading

Bateson, Gregory and Mead, Margaret: *Balinese Character,* New York Academy of Sciences, 1942.

Freeman, Derek: *Margaret Mead and Samoa,* Cambridge Massachusetts and London: Harvard University Press, 1983.

Mead, Margaret: *Blackberry Winter,* Angus and Robertson, London, 1973.

Coming of Age in Samoa, Morrow, New York, 1928; Jonathan Cape, London, 1929.

Growing Up in New Guinea, Morrow, New York, 1930; Routledge, London, 1931.

Letters from the Field, 1925-1975, Harper and Row, London and New York, 1977.

Sex and Temperament in Three Primitive Societies, Morrow, New York, 1935; Routledge, London, 1935.

Anthropological Terms:

Adolescence: The period of growing up between childhood and adulthood.

Anthropology: The scientific study of the human race, in particular its origin, physical development, customs, societies and the way it behaves.

Child development: The process of growing and learning.

Extended family: A family group living together that includes grandparents, parents, children and other close relatives, such as aunts, uncles and cousins.

Free love: Sexual relations without the commitment of marriage or any formal or legal obligations.

Illiterate: Being unable to read or write.

Intellectual: Being able to learn, think and reason. Also, someone who has a high level of intelligence.

Kinship: Human relationship that is based on blood or marriage. Most human societies and social groupings are founded on kinship and strict social customs, rules and taboos have evolved.

Native: Belonging by origin or birth to a particular place or country.

Nature: The effects of heredity as an influence on someone's personality.

Nurture: The effects of upbringing and the human environment on someone's personality.

Primitive: Relating to the early stages of civilization.

Social security: Financial help, provided by the state, for those in need – in particular, the elderly, poor, disabled, sick and unemployed.

Taboo: Something that is prohibited by tradition or social custom.

Temperament: The way a person acts, feels and thinks.

Under-developed: Relating to a country, one that is poor and in need of aid from richer nations.

"From my own first field trip to Samoa participation has involved entering into many facets of the life of the people I have worked among – eating the food, learning to weave a mat or make a gesture of respect or prepare an offering or recite a charm as they had been taught to do ... as one further way of coming to understand the people who were my teachers as well as the subjects of my study." Margaret Mead, from "Letters from the Field".

"In the 1920s we knew that primitive societies were vanishing. Today we know that those still remaining are being destroyed even more rapidly by the overpowering impact of our technological society.... Nevertheless, there are still, in remote parts of the world, living primitive societies."
Margaret Mead, from her autobiography, "Blackberry Winter".

"It was on a trip with Margaret many years ago that I learned that humanity is indeed a family. I hope that people all over the world, when they look at [this collection of my] photographs, will realize they share similar experiences. Then they might think, 'This is our world, we better take care of it.'"
Ken Heyman.

Index